ZEBRAS

A TRUE BOOK

by
Melissa Stewart

Children's Press®
A Division of Scholastic Inc.

New York Toronto London Auckland Sydney
Mexico City New Delhi Hong Kong
Danbury, Connecticut

Zebras grooming
themselves on a rock

Reading Consultant
Nanci R. Vargus, Ed.D.
Primary Multiage Teacher
Decatur Township Schools,
Indianapolis, Indiana

Content Consultant
Kathy Carlstead, Ph.D.
Honolulu Zoo

Dedication:
To Colin Campbell Stewart

Library of Congress Cataloging-in-Publication Data

Stewart, Melissa
    Zebras / by Melissa Stewart.
        p.   cm. — (A true book)
    Includes bibliographical references and index.
    Summary: An overview of the physical characteristics, behavior, habitat, and different varieties of zebras.
    ISBN 0-516-22203-1 (lib. bdg.)   0-516-26993-3 (pbk.)
    1. Zebras—Juvenile literature. [1. Zebras] I. Title. II. Series.
QL737.U62 S745 2002
599.665'7—dc21   2001047197

Contents

Zebras drinking
at a water hole

A Zebra's Life

It's early morning in Africa, and a zebra herd is just waking up. After a long, cool drink at a nearby water hole, the animals begin to graze. They will spend most of the day snipping tall, coarse grasses with their sharp front

A zebra uses its tough molars to grind its food.

teeth and grinding the plants with their tough molars.

Sometimes zebras must travel up to 30 miles (48 kilometers) a day in search of food and water, but not today. It is the wet season, and food is plentiful.

Zebras are always alert. Even when they eat, they focus on the grass with one part of their

Zebras and wildebeest grazing

eye and look out for danger with the other part of their eye. All the while, their cup-shaped ears swivel back and forth. When zebras rest or groom one another, they usually face in opposite directions, so they can spot enemies.

It is very hard for a predator to sneak up on a zebra. A hungry lion must hide patiently in tall grass and wait for a zebra to stray from its herd. Then the lion pounces on the animal

When zebras groom each other, they face in opposite directions so they can spot enemies.

A lion hunting a zebra

and bites its neck, killing it instantly. Most of the time, hyenas and jackals attack zebras that are very young, very old, or sick.

When a zebra detects an enemy, it lets out a sharp warning bark, kicks at the predator with its strong back legs, and then takes off at top speed. A zebra has a strong heart and lungs and muscular legs. It can gallop as fast as 37 miles (60 km) per hour.

Zebras have many enemies, so they must always be ready to flee from danger.

When zebras run in a group, their stripes blend together. It may be hard for enemies to tell where one zebra ends and another starts.

In the evening, most of the herd goes to sleep. But one zebra always stays awake and watches for leopards and other enemies. Even at night, the entire herd must be ready to flee at a moment's notice.

Keeping Clean

Dirt and flaking skin often get caught in a zebra's fur, and insects burrow into its skin. To keep their fur clean, zebras spend a lot of time grooming themselves—and each other. They spend a few hours every day licking and biting at their skin and fur.

If they have trouble reaching a spot, zebras may roll around on the ground or rub against rocks, stumps, and each other. Sometimes they even take dust baths. A thin layer of dust also protects a zebra's skin from the sun.

Zebra Families

A family of zebras usually has between five and twenty members. The family has only one adult male, or stallion. He is the leader. The family also includes up to six adult females, or mares, and their young. Baby zebras are called foals. Young male zebras are

A family of zebras

called colts, and young
females are called fillies.

17

When zebras travel,
the oldest female
leads the group.

Most mares stay with the same family all their life. They mate only with the leader of their family. When the family travels, the oldest female leads while the male walks at the rear of the group.

If a male from another family approaches a filly, the leader pulls back his lips and shows his sharp teeth. He stomps his feet, flattens his ears, and snorts loudly. He is challenging the intruder to a fight. If the

Male zebras fighting

intruder does not back down, the two males start to bite and kick each other. They also wrestle with their necks. Finally, one animal surrenders by lowering his head and backing away.

Sometimes zebra families join together to form huge herds of zebras. Yet within these large groups, the zebras still maintain close ties with their family members.

Can you count how many zebras are in this herd?

All About Zebras

Most zebras are white with black stripes. But no two zebras have the same pattern of stripes. Just as you can identify a person by his or her fingerprints, you can identify a zebra by its stripes.

Zebras are closely related to horses. Both zebras and

Can you see how each zebra has a different pattern of stripes?

Zebras are closely related to horses.

horses eat plants and can gallop at high speeds. The feet of both have one toe that is protected by a thick, tough hoof. Horses and zebras belong to a larger group of animals called mammals. Cows, mice, elephants, and humans are also mammals.

All mammals have a backbone that supports their body and helps them move. They also have lungs and breathe air. They are warm blooded, so their body temperature stays about the same no matter how cold or warm their environment is. Many mammals have four legs and a hairy body.

Female mammals give birth to live babies and feed them with mother's milk. A baby zebra, or foal, has soft, fuzzy fur with brown and tan stripes. It can stand 10 minutes after it

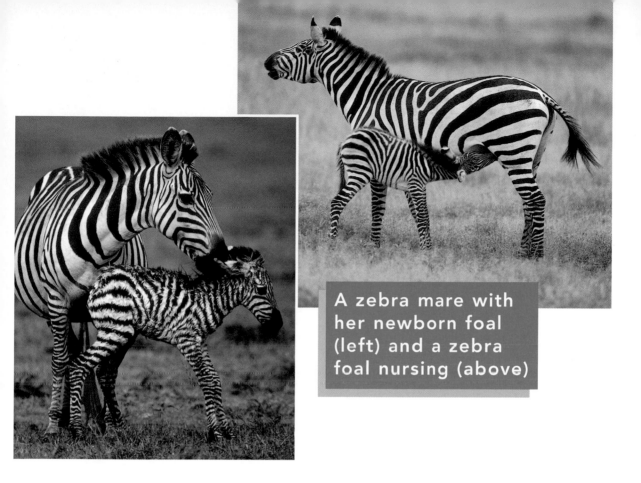

A zebra mare with her newborn foal (left) and a zebra foal nursing (above)

is born and can run an hour later. Although the youngster will keep drinking milk for up to a year, it starts to eat some grass when it is only a week old.

Zebras at play

When a zebra is about 4 months old, it begins to play with other youngsters. They push and shove, race, and play tag. They are learning skills that will help them survive as adults. Young zebras must also learn to obey herd rules.

When a mare is about 2 1/2 years old, she can start to have young of her own. At about the same time, young males leave their herd and join a group of males. Most males do not start to mate until they are 5 or 6 years old.

Three Kinds of Zebras

There are three different kinds of zebras in the world—Grévy's, mountain, and Burchell's. The largest zebra, Grévy's zebra, lives in northern Kenya, Somalia, Ethiopia, and the Sudan. It was named after Jules Grévy, the president of France in the late 1800s.

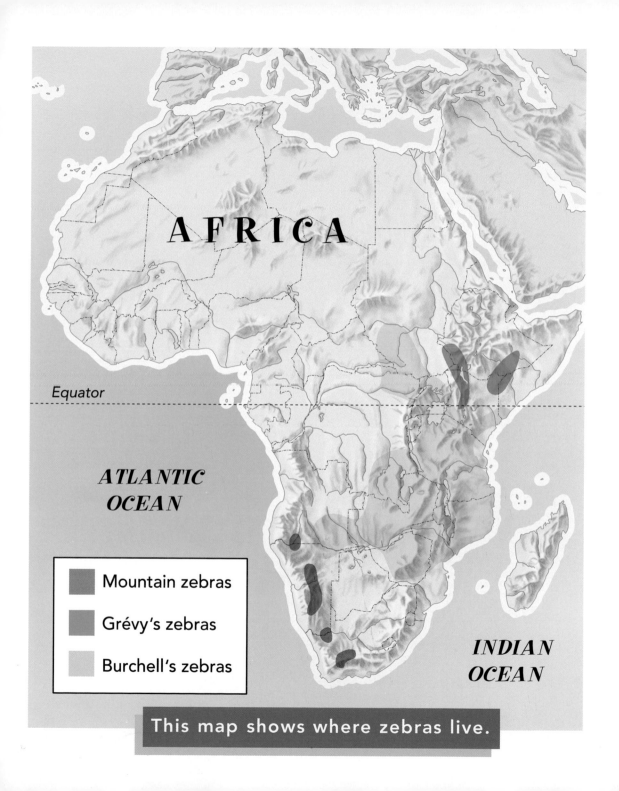

AFRICA

Equator

ATLANTIC
OCEAN

INDIAN
OCEAN

Mountain zebras

Grévy's zebras

Burchell's zebras

This map shows where zebras live.

Each Grévy's zebra has narrow stripes, a white belly, and a black stripe running down its back.

Grévy's zebra is about 5 feet (1.5 meters) high at the shoulder and weighs 780 to 950 pounds (354 to 431 kilograms). It has rounded ears, a long tail, narrow black stripes, and a white belly. A single black stripe runs down its back from its mane to its tail. This zebra brays like a mule, and usually lives alone or in small temporary groups.

The mountain zebra lives in southern Africa. It is just 4 feet (1.2 m) tall at the shoulder and

A mountain zebra and foal

weighs about 600 pounds (272 kg). This plump little animal has a long head with pointed ears, a brown muzzle, and a loose flap of skin under

The mountain zebra lives in dry, stony, hilly areas of southern Africa.

its chin. It also has a short tuft of hair on its tail. The mountain zebra's thin legs and narrow hooves help it climb up dry, stony hills and rocky cliffs.

Burchell's zebras (above), also called plains zebras, are the most common zebra in the world. Some plains zebras have light "shadow" stripes in between the dark, wide ones.

Burchell's zebra, also called the plains zebra, is the most common zebra in zoos and in the wild. It lives on the grassy plains and in the woodlands of central and East Africa. Each year, these zebras travel hundreds of miles in search of food.

A Burchell's zebra is about 4.5 feet (1.4 m) tall at the shoulder and weighs about 700 pounds (318 kg). It has wide stripes, a black muzzle, thick short legs, large hooves, and long tail. Some plains zebras have light, thin "shadow" stripes between the dark, wide ones.

Zebras in Danger

Zebras have many predators, but humans are their most dangerous enemy. For hundreds of years, human hunters have killed zebras for their meat. Their hides can be tanned into leather and used to make shoes, rugs, chair coverings, clothing, and other products.

Zebras have long been hunted for their skins.

These mountain zebras live at Mountain Zebra National Park in South Africa.

Even though zebras have been so widely hunted, some kinds are still quite common. But mountain zebras are in great danger. Most mountain zebras live in special parks where they are protected from hunters and their habitat is protected from farmers and builders.

Although zebras are better off than many other African animals, that could change very quickly. Many years ago

At one time quaggas were common in South Africa. The last ones died out in the late 1800s.

the quagga, a close relative of the zebra, vanished from Earth forever. If we do not protect zebras and the places where they live, these amazing striped creatures may die out too.

How long will zebras be part of our world?

To Find Out More

Here are some additional resources to help you learn more about zebras:

 **Books**

Fredericks, Anthony D. **Zebras.** Lerner, 2000.

Huot-Denis, Christine. **The Zebra: Striped Horse.** Charlesbridge, 1999.

Patent, Dorothy Hinshaw. **Why Mammals Have Fur.** New York: Cobble Hill Books, 1995.

Stewart, Melissa. **Mammals.** Children's Press, 2001.

Organizations and Online Sites

African Wildlife Update
4739 Fox Trail Dr. NE
Olympia, Washington
98516
*http://www.africanwildlife.
org/*

Get up-to-the-minute information about the status of
zebras and other animals
that live in Africa.

Grant's Zebra
*http://www.oaklandzoo.org
/atoz/azebra.html*

The Grant's zebra is a kind
of Burchell's zebra. At this
Web site, you can hear the
sounds they make and
watch movies of the zebras
at the Oakland Zoo in
California. You also can
read basic information
about what these zebras
eat and how they spend
their days.

**Herds of Information
About Zebras**
*http://www.alumni.caltech
.edu/~kantner/zebras/*

This site features photos
and descriptions of the
three different kinds of
zebras. There are also plen-
ty of links to other interest-
ing sites.

**International Wildlife
Coalition**
70 East Falmouth Highway
East Falmouth, MA, USA
02536
http://www.iwc.org

The IWC works to save
endangered species and
preserve animal habitats
and the environment.

KidsGoWild
*http://wcs.org/sites/
kidsgowild*

This is the kids' page of the
Wildlife Conservation
Society. It includes wildlife
news, wild animal facts,
and information on how
kids can get involved in
saving wild animals and the
environment by joining
Conservation Kids.

Important Words

detect to notice, find

graze to eat grass

groom to clean skin or fur by licking, biting, or rubbing

habitat place where a creature lives

maintain to keep something going

mammal warm-blooded animal that has a backbone and fur and feeds its young with mother's milk

molar kind of tooth a zebra uses to grind grasses and other plants

muzzle the nose and mouth of an animal, snout

predator animal that hunts and kills other animals for food

savanna grassy plain

Index

Meet the Author

A few years ago, Melissa Stewart visited the African countries of Kenya and Tanzania. While on safari, she saw many Burchell's and Grévy's zebras. Like lions and other predators, she had trouble making out individual zebras when spooked herds were on the run.

Ms. Stewart earned a bachelor's degree in biology from Union College and a master's degree in science and environmental journalism from New York University. The inspiration for many of the children's books she has written comes from her travels, but she also enjoys spending time observing the wildlife near her home in Marlborough, Massachusetts.